Christmas Cookies and Candy

GRAMERCY BOOKS
New York • Avenel

Copyright © 1995 by
Random House Value Publishing, Inc.
All rights reserved.

This edition is published by Gramercy Books,
distributed by Random House Value Publishing, Inc.
40 Engelhard Avenue
Avenel, New Jersey 07001

Random House
New York • Toronto • London • Sydney • Auckland

Printed and bound in Italy

Library of Congress Cataloging-in-Publication Data
Christmas cookies and candy.

p.   cm.
ISBN 0-517-12438-6
1. Cookies.   2. Candy.   3. Christmas cookery.
TX772.C484   1995
641.8'654—dc20   95-17789
                                             CIP

8 7 6 5 4 3 2 1

Christmas Cookies

Christmas Cookies
Contents

Introduction	11
Baking the Best Cookies	12
Storing Cookies	13
Packaging Cookies	13
Mailing Cookies	14
Cutout Cookies	15
Painted Cookies	16
Christmas Wreaths	18
Lebkuchen	20
Stained-Glass Window Cookies	22
Gingerbread People and Things	24
Orange Butter Cookies	26
Drop Cookies	27
Pumpkin Cookies	28
Brown-Edged Cookies	30
Monster Peanut Butter Cookies	31
Chocolate Meringues	32
Oatmeal Lace Cookies	33
Pecan Clusters	34
Hermits	35
Walnut Rocks	36

Orange Drop Cookies   37
Coconut Cornflake Cookies   38

Bar Cookies   39
Holiday Layer Squares   40
Fudge Brownies   41
Spicy Molasses Bars   42
Pumpkin Shortbread Squares   43
Chocolate Chip Squares   44

Hand-Shaped Cookies   45
Chocolate Teddy Bears   46
Walnut Cookie Balls   48
Peppernuts   49
Spicy Chocolate Cookies   50
Pecan Spice Cookies   51
Chocolate Chocolate Cookies   52
Date Walnut Cookies   53
Chocolate Crackles   54
Sandies   55
Gingersnaps   56

Special Cookies   57
Spritz Cookies   58
Chocolate Spritz Ribbons   59
Pecan Pie Cookies   60
Christmas Fantasy Cookies   61
Miniature Fruitcakes   62

Introduction

Rich melted chocolate and fragrant vanilla, crunchy nuts and chewy dates, spicy cinnamon and ginger, tangy orange and lemon rind—these are the delights of Christmas, when the kitchen is warm with remembered smells and flavors and the cookie jar is always full.

Cookies and Christmas seem to be synonymous. Perhaps this is because cookies are so versatile. Packed in a bright tin, a basket, or even a patterned paper bag, they make a thoughtful gift for a neighbor or hostess. Cookies can be used as ornaments on the Christmas tree or as personalized labels on packages. A beautifully arranged platter of cookies is a wonderful addition to a buffet table, and no one can resist a cookie that accompanies an ice cream or fruit dessert. Best of all, most cookies are easy to make, and while they are baking they fill the whole house with a delicious aroma.

Here is a new collection of irresistible cookie recipes. There are instructions for baking bar cookies and drop cookies, hand-shaped cookies and cutouts. You'll find recipes for painted cookies and gingerbread people, pumpkin cookies and chocolate teddy bears, miniature fruitcakes and tiny pecan pies, orange drop cookies and chocolate meringues. You'll want to try them all—and keep your cookie jar filled not just for the holidays, but all through the year.

Baking the Best Cookies

Just follow these ten basic rules and you will always bake wonderful cookies:

♠ Always read a recipe through from beginning to end before starting to bake. You will then be sure to have all the necessary ingredients on hand, as well as sufficient time.

♠ Always use the best-quality, freshest ingredients available.

♠ Measure ingredients accurately, using standard measuring spoons for small amounts, a fluid measuring cup for liquids, and graduated measuring cups for dry ingredients.

♠ Follow recipes carefully. Use only the ingredients specified and add them in the order and by the method given in the recipe.

♠ Always preheat the oven for at least 15 minutes at the required temperature.

♠ Try to make all the cookies in a batch the same size and thickness so they will bake evenly.

♠ It is best to bake only one sheet of cookies at a time on an oven rack in the upper third of the oven. If you must bake two sheets of cookies at a time, place the second oven rack as close as possible below the first and place the cookie sheets so that neither is directly above or below the other. To ensure even baking, reverse the position of the cookie sheets halfway through the baking time.

♠ Always use a timer for accuracy.

♠ Unless a recipe directs you to do otherwise, as soon as you take the cookie sheet out of the oven remove the cookies with a spatula and transfer them to wire racks to cool completely.

♠ Before placing another batch of cookies on the cookie sheet, let it cool, then brush off any crumbs. It is not necessary to grease the sheet again.

Storing Cookies

Cookies keep well if they are stored properly. Consequently, they can be made several days in advance of the occasion at which they will be served. They are perfect as gifts and can even be mailed to faraway places. Here are some rules for storing cookies so that they remain as delicious as they are when they come out of the oven:

🌲 Always allow cookies to cool thoroughly before storing.

🌲 Store soft cookies in a container with a tight-fitting lid. To restore moisture to soft cookies that have begun to dry out, place a piece of bread or a wedge of raw apple in the container with the cookies for 24 hours.

🌲 Bar cookies may be stored in the pan in which they were baked, tightly covered with foil or plastic wrap.

🌲 Crisp cookies should be stored in a container with a loose-fitting lid. If they soften, put them in a 300°F oven for 5 minutes before serving.

🌲 Store moist and crisp cookies separately. If they are stored together, the crisp cookies will get soggy.

🌲 Cookies made from very buttery dough should be stored in the refrigerator in an airtight container.

🌲 Baked cookies may be frozen in freezer containers or tightly closed plastic bags for up to 12 months. Thaw them at room temperature for 15 minutes before serving.

Packaging Cookies

Cookies make splendid gifts, and wrapped imaginatively they can be very special. Attractive tins and wooden or cardboard boxes make fine containers for cookies. And what could be a more appropriate gift container than a cookie jar?

When using a round wooden box or tin, line it with several layers of white doilies. Cut rounds of waxed paper a little

smaller than the circumference of the box. Put several thicknesses of the paper between each layer of cookies. Put a piece of waxed paper, then a doily, on top. Tie a ribbon crosswise around the closed box.

A wide-mouthed glass jar that has a well-fitting lid can be neatly filled with an assortment of cookies. Wrap the jar using several layers of colored tissue paper. Gather the tissue paper at the top with curling ribbon.

Baskets make excellent containers for cookies. Line the basket with white paper doilies. Arrange the cookies in the basket; they'll look best if you cluster the same kinds of cookies together. Wrap the whole basket in cellophane and tie a bright ribbon around it.

Mailing Cookies

Soft, moist bar and drop cookies, brownies, and miniature fruitcakes travel best through the mail. Thin, crisp cookies tend to crumble easily and frosted cookies often become sticky.

Use a sturdy, heavy cardboard box and have on hand an ample supply of such filler material as bubble wrap, crumpled foil, waxed paper, tissue paper, or paper towels. Begin by lining the box with foil or plastic wrap. Then put a layer of filler in the bottom of the box.

Wrap cookies individually or back to back in foil or plastic wrap, then pack the cookies in neat rows with filler between the rows and layers. When sending an assortment of cookies, put the heaviest ones on the bottom. Be sure the box is full enough to prevent the contents moving when the box is closed and put a generous layer of filler on top of the top layer of cookies. Alternatively, pack the cookies in layers in a decorative tin, using lots of filler. Tape the tin closed, then put it into a well-padded box for mailing and wrap it securely.

Be sure to mark the package FRAGILE and PERISHABLE.

Cutout Cookies

Cutout cookies are always fun to make because there is such a variety of cookie cutters available and so many ways that the cookies can be decorated. The recipes in this section will give you lots of inspiration.

The dough for cutout cookies must be firm so it won't stick to the rolling pin or work surface. For this reason, it should be chilled in the refrigerator for several hours or overnight. For faster chilling, divide the dough in half, or even in quarters, and wrap each portion in foil or plastic wrap before putting it into the refrigerator. Roll out only one portion of the dough at a time and keep the rest in the refrigerator.

Roll the dough on a lightly floured surface using a floured rolling pin. Always roll from the edges to the center. Cookie cutters should be dusted with flour or confectioners' sugar so they won't stick. Cut out the cookies as close together as possible, then lift them with a spatula and place them on the cookie sheets.

Unless a recipe specifies otherwise, cutout cookies should be baked only until they are very lightly browned around the edges.

Painted Cookies

These cookies are decorated with brightly colored egg-yolk paint that is applied with artists' paintbrushes before the cookies are baked. The best effects are achieved when the paint is used as an accent, rather than as a covering for a whole cookie. This recipe can also be used to make cookie labels for presents. Follow the recipe, but roll out the dough to a thickness of $\frac{1}{4}$ inch. Cut out the cookies in rectangles. Before baking, make a hole on one side with a drinking straw. Then use the egg-yolk paint to decorate the labels and paint on the names. The labels can be tied to packages with thin ribbon or yarn.

Makes about 70 cookies

> 1 cup unsalted butter, at room temperature
> 2 cups granulated sugar
> 2 eggs
> 1 teaspoon lemon extract
> $\frac{1}{2}$ teaspoon baking soda
> 1 cup commercial sour cream
> 5 cups all-purpose flour
>
> Egg-Yolk Paint
> 2 egg yolks
> $\frac{1}{2}$ teaspoon water
> Food coloring

In a large mixing bowl, cream the butter until it is smooth. Add the sugar and beat until light and fluffy. Add the eggs, one at a time, and beat well. Beat in the lemon extract.

Combine the baking soda with the sour cream. Add the flour to the batter, $\frac{1}{2}$ cup at a time, alternating with the sour-cream mixture and mixing well after each addition.

Gather the dough into two balls. Wrap each in foil and chill in the refrigerator for 2 hours.

Preheat the oven to 400°F. Lightly grease cookie sheets with butter.

On a lightly floured surface, roll out half the dough to a thickness of $\frac{1}{8}$ inch. (Keep the rest of the dough chilled until needed.) Cut out the dough with a variety of cookie cutters. Reroll and cut the scraps. Place the cookies on the prepared cookie sheets.

To make the egg-yolk paint, using a fork, blend the egg yolks with the water. Divide the mixture into small bowls. Tint each portion with sufficient food coloring to color it brightly.

Paint the cookies as desired, using a separate paintbrush for each color. If the paint thickens while standing, thin it with a few drops of water.

Bake the cookies for 8 to 10 minutes, or until the edges are lightly browned.

Christmas Wreaths

These delicate, pretty cookies make wonderful decorations for the tree. Use tiny cinnamon candies or red gumdrops to make the holly berries.

Makes about 60 cookies

$\frac{3}{4}$ cup unsalted butter, at room temperature
1 cup granulated sugar
1 egg
1 teaspoon vanilla extract
3 cups all-purpose flour
1 teaspoon baking soda
$\frac{1}{2}$ teaspoon salt
Red candies

Decorative Icing
1 pound-package confectioners' sugar
6 tablespoons water
Green food coloring

In a large mixing bowl, cream together the butter and sugar, then beat until the mixture is fluffy. Beat in the egg and the vanilla.

Sift together the flour, baking soda, and salt. Add to the batter, $\frac{1}{2}$ cup at a time, blending well after each addition.

Gather the dough into two balls. Wrap each in foil and chill in the refrigerator overnight.

Preheat the oven to 350°F.

On a lightly floured surface, roll out half the dough to a thickness of $\frac{1}{4}$ inch. (Keep the rest of the dough chilled until needed.) Cut out the dough with a 3-inch round cookie cutter, then cut out the centers with a 1-inch round cutter. Reroll and cut the scraps.

Place the cookies on ungreased cookie sheets. Bake for 10 minutes, or until the cookies are lightly browned around the edges. Cool the cookies on wire racks.

To make the icing, sift the confectioners' sugar into a medium bowl. Add the water, 1 tablespoon at a time, beating until the mixture is smooth. Add a few drops of green food coloring and blend well. If the icing is too stiff, add a little more water, a few drops at a time.

When the cookies are completely cool, swirl the icing on them, then decorate with the red candies.

Lebkuchen

These spicy honey cookies have been part of the German Christmas tradition for hundreds of years. There are many recipes for lebkuchen. This is one of the best.

Makes about 90 cookies

1 cup honey
2 eggs
$\frac{3}{4}$ cup firmly packed dark brown sugar
1 tablespoon lemon juice
1 teaspoon grated lemon rind
2$\frac{3}{4}$ cups all-purpose flour
1$\frac{1}{2}$ teaspoons baking soda
1 teaspoon ground cinnamon
1 teaspoon ground allspice
$\frac{1}{2}$ teaspoon ground nutmeg
$\frac{1}{4}$ teaspoon ground cloves
$\frac{1}{3}$ cup finely chopped citron
$\frac{1}{3}$ cup finely chopped walnuts
2 tablespoons milk

Cookie Glaze
1 teaspoon cornstarch
$\frac{1}{4}$ cup confectioners' sugar
$\frac{1}{2}$ cup granulated sugar
$\frac{1}{4}$ cup water

In a small saucepan, heat the honey just until it simmers. Remove the pan from the heat and set aside to cool.

In a large mixing bowl, beat 1 egg until foamy. Add the sugar, $\frac{1}{4}$ cup at a time, beating well after each addition. Add the honey, the lemon juice, and the grated lemon rind and mix well.

Sift together the flour, baking soda, cinnamon, allspice, nutmeg, and cloves. Blend the sifted ingredients into the honey mixture. Add the citron and the nuts and mix well.

Divide the dough into four parts. Wrap each in foil and chill in the refrigerator overnight.

Preheat the oven to 400°F. Lightly grease cookie sheets with butter. Lightly beat the remaining egg with the milk.

Make the cookie glaze. Sift together the cornstarch and the confectioners' sugar. Set aside. In a saucepan, combine the granulated sugar and the water. Bring to a boil, stirring constantly until the sugar dissolves. Continue boiling until the mixture threads from the spoon (230°F on a candy thermometer). Remove the pan from the heat and gradually stir in the confectioners'-sugar mixture. Set aside.

On a lightly floured surface, roll out one-quarter of the dough to a thickness of $\frac{1}{4}$ inch. (Keep the rest of the dough chilled until ready to use.) Cut the dough using a 2-inch round cookie cutter. Reroll and cut the scraps.

Place the cookies 1 inch apart on the prepared cookie sheets. Brush each one with the egg and milk mixture. Bake for 10 to 12 minutes, or until no indentations remain on the cookies when touched.

When the lebkuchen are removed from the oven, immediately brush them with the glaze. (If the glaze crystallizes while brushing the cookies, warm it over low heat, adding a little water, until it is clear again.) Transfer the cookies to wire racks to cool.

Stained-Glass Window Cookies

These cookies are so lovely you may want to hang some of them on your Christmas tree. To make cookie ornaments, use a drinking straw to make a hole in the top end of each cookie before baking it. After the cookies have cooled completely, simply thread a piece of yarn through each hole, tying the yarn at the top to make a loop. The hard candy required in this recipe can be sour balls in assorted colors or you may use rolls of ring-shaped candy.

Makes about 40 cookies

    6 *tablespoons unsalted butter, at room temperature*
    $\frac{1}{3}$ *cup shortening*
    $\frac{3}{4}$ *cup granulated sugar*
    1 *egg*
    1 *tablespoon milk*
    1 *teaspoon vanilla extract*
    2 *cups all-purpose flour*
    $1\frac{1}{2}$ *teaspoons baking powder*
    $\frac{1}{4}$ *teaspoon salt*
    4 *ounces hard candy*

In a large mixing bowl, cream together the butter, shortening, and sugar. Beat until light and fluffy. Beat in the egg, the milk, and the vanilla.

Sift together the flour, baking powder, and salt. Add the sifted ingredients, $\frac{1}{2}$ cup at a time, to the batter. Beat until smooth.

Divide the dough in half. Wrap each half in foil and chill in the refrigerator for at least 3 hours.

Preheat the oven to 375°F. Line cookie sheets with foil.

On a lightly floured surface, roll out half the dough to a thickness of $\frac{1}{8}$ inch. (Keep the rest of the dough chilled until needed.) Cut with decorative cookie cutters. Reroll and cut the scraps.

Place the cookies on the lined cookie sheets. Using a sharp knife or tiny hors d'oeuvre cutters, carefully cut out one or more small shapes in the middle of each cookie.

Separate the hard candies by color and put them into plastic bags. Place one bag at a time in a dish towel and, using a hammer or the flat edge of a meat mallet, crush the candy into coarse pieces.

Spoon a little of the candy into the cutout centers of the cookies. Be sure to fill the holes to the level of the dough. (As the cookies bake the candy will melt into smooth windows.)

Bake the cookies for 7 minutes, or until the edges of the cookies are lightly browned and the candy has melted.

Let the cookies cool completely on the cookie sheet, then remove them carefully with a spatula.

Gingerbread People and Things

Boys and girls, Christmas trees and wreaths, stars and crescent moons—this recipe can be used to make whatever manner of cutout gingerbread cookie you choose.

Makes about sixty 6-inch cookies or ninety 3-inch cookies

5 cups all-purpose flour
1½ teaspoons baking soda
2 teaspoons ground ginger
1 teaspoon ground cinnamon
1 teaspoon ground cloves
½ teaspoon salt
1 cup shortening
1 cup granulated sugar
1 egg
1 cup molasses
2 tablespoons white vinegar

Decorative Icing
1 egg white
2 teaspoons lemon juice
1½ to 2 cups confectioners' sugar, sifted
Food coloring

Sift together the flour, baking soda, ginger, cinnamon, cloves, and salt.

In a large mixing bowl, beat the shortening until it is soft and smooth. Add the sugar and beat until the mixture is fluffy. Add the egg, molasses, and vinegar. Beat well. Add the flour mixture, ½ cup at a time, beating well after each addition. When the dough is smooth, divide it into quarters. Wrap each portion in foil and chill in the refrigerator for at least 3 hours.

Preheat the oven to 375°F. Grease cookie sheets with butter. On a lightly floured surface, roll out the dough to a thickness of $\frac{1}{8}$ inch. (Use only one-quarter of the dough at a time and keep the remainder in the refrigerator until you are ready to use it.) Cut the dough with cookie cutters. Reroll and cut the scraps.

Place the cookies on the cookie sheets. Bake for 5 minutes, or until the cookies are very lightly browned around the edges.

Let the cookies cool on the cookie sheets for 1 minute, then transfer them to wire racks to cool completely.

To make the icing, in a small mixing bowl, beat the egg white, lemon juice, and 1 cup of the confectioners' sugar. Gradually add only enough confectioners' sugar to make an icing of piping consistency. When the consistency seems right, stir in a few drops of food coloring if desired.

To decorate the cookies, fill a decorating bag no more than half full of icing. Use a tip with a small opening. First pipe outlines on the edges of the cookies, then fill in the details.

Orange Butter Cookies

Use a variety of cookie cutters to make these delicious cookies.
Store them in airtight containers in the refrigerator.

Makes about sixty 2-inch cookies

> 2 cups unsalted butter, at room temperature
> 1½ cups firmly packed light brown sugar
> 4 cups all-purpose flour
> ⅛ teaspoon salt
> 2 large navel oranges
> 2 eggs
> 2 tablespoons water

In a large mixing bowl, cream the butter and sugar together.
Gradually beat in the flour, ½ cup at a time. Add the salt and
mix well. Grate the rind of the oranges and mix it into the
dough.

Gather the dough into a ball, wrap it in foil, and chill it in
the refrigerator for at least 4 hours.

Preheat the oven to 350°F. Line cookie sheets with baking
parchment.

On a lightly floured surface, roll out the dough to a thickness
of ½ inch. Cut out the cookies using a variety of 2-inch cookie
cutters. Reroll and cut the scraps.

In a small bowl, beat the eggs and water together. Place the
cookies on the prepared cookie sheets. Brush the egg mixture
lightly over the cookies. Bake for 15 to 20 minutes, or until the
cookies are a light golden brown.

Drop Cookies

Drop cookies are so named because spoonfuls of the soft dough are dropped onto the cookie sheet in mounds that spread when baked. There the similarity ends. Drop cookies may be crisp or chewy, plain, or full of fruit and nuts and other goodies.

Since the dough for drop cookies spreads as it bakes, always use cool cookie sheets to prevent excessive spreading.

It is helpful to use the tip of a table knife or another spoon to push the dough off the spoon onto the cookie sheet. Try to make all the cookies the same size so they will bake evenly.

Drop cookies are done when the dough is set, the bottoms are lightly browned (check by using a table knife or a metal spatula to lift a cookie so you can peek underneath), and the tops look dry rather than shiny.

Pumpkin Cookies

Delicately spiced and full of dates and nuts, these cookies are wonderful plain and even better when they are frosted with an orange icing.

Makes about 36 cookies

1 cup unsalted butter, at room temperature
1 cup granulated sugar
1 egg, lightly beaten
1 teaspoon vanilla extract
1 cup canned pumpkin puree
2 cups all-purpose flour
1 teaspoon baking powder
1 teaspoon baking soda
$\frac{1}{2}$ teaspoon salt
1 teaspoon ground cinnamon
$\frac{1}{4}$ teaspoon ground nutmeg
$\frac{1}{4}$ teaspoon ground cloves
1 cup finely chopped dates
$\frac{1}{2}$ cup finely chopped walnuts

Orange Icing
$\frac{1}{3}$ cup unsalted butter, at room temperature
2 cups confectioners' sugar
2 to 3 tablespoons orange juice

Preheat the oven to 350°F.

In a large mixing bowl, cream together the butter and sugar. Add the egg and vanilla and beat well. Beat in the pumpkin puree.

Sift together the flour, baking powder, baking soda, salt, cinnamon, nutmeg, and cloves. Add the sifted ingredients to the batter, $\frac{1}{2}$ cup at a time, mixing well after each addition. Stir in the dates and the walnuts.

Drop by teaspoonfuls, about 2 inches apart, onto ungreased cookie sheets. Bake for 12 to 15 minutes, or until the cookies are firm and the bottoms are lightly browned. Transfer the cookies to wire racks to cool completely.

To make the icing, in a large mixing bowl, cream together the butter and the sugar. Beat in the orange juice, 1 tablespoon at a time, until the frosting is of a spreading consistency.

Using a spatula, swirl the icing on top of each cookie.

Brown-Edged Cookies

These classic cookies are easy to make and always delicious. Pecans or candied cherry halves may be substituted for the walnuts.

Makes about 75 cookies

> 1 cup unsalted butter, at room temperature
> 2 teaspoons salt
> 1 teaspoon vanilla extract
> $\frac{2}{3}$ cup granulated sugar
> 1 egg
> $2\frac{1}{2}$ cups sifted all-purpose flour
> $\frac{1}{2}$ cup light cream
> Confectioners' sugar
> Walnut halves

Preheat the oven to 375°F. Lightly grease cookie sheets with butter.

In a large mixing bowl, cream together the butter, salt, vanilla, and sugar, then beat until the mixture is light and fluffy. Beat in the egg. Add the flour, $\frac{1}{2}$ cup at a time, alternating with the cream. Beat well after each addition.

Drop the batter by teaspoonfuls, about 2 inches apart, onto the prepared cookie sheets. Let stand for 3 minutes.

Dip the bottom of a glass into confectioners' sugar, then use it to press the cookies flat. Gently press a walnut half into the center of each cookie.

Bake for 8 minutes, or until the edges of the cookies are lightly browned.

Monster Peanut Butter Cookies

Kids are amused and delighted by cookies that are the size of small plates. They love to eat them and to make them themselves. This recipe makes twelve 6-inch cookies. Double or triple the ingredients to increase the number. Any favorite drop cookie recipe, perhaps for oatmeal or chocolate chip cookies, can be used to make "monsters." Just use $\frac{1}{3}$ cup of dough for each cookie.

Makes 12 large cookies

> 1 cup unsalted butter, at room temperature
> 1 cup granulated sugar
> 1 cup chunky peanut butter
> 2$\frac{1}{2}$ cups all-purpose flour
> Confectioners' sugar

Preheat the oven to 375°F. Liberally grease cookie sheets with butter.

In a large mixing bowl, cream together the butter and sugar, then beat until the mixture is light and fluffy. Beat in the peanut butter. Add the flour, $\frac{1}{2}$ cup at a time, and mix well.

Scoop up $\frac{1}{3}$-cup measures of the dough and drop on the prepared cookie sheets. (The dough will spread, so it probably will not be possible to bake more than four cookies on one sheet.) Dip the bottom of a pie plate in confectioners' sugar and use it to press each mound firmly so that it flattens into a 6-inch circle.

Bake the cookies for 15 minutes.

Let the cookies cool on the cookie sheets for at least 5 minutes, then use a pancake turner to transfer them to wire racks to cool completely.

Chocolate Meringues

Crisp and delicate, these little meringues melt in the mouth. They are a delightful addition to a platter of Christmas goodies.

Makes about 96 small meringues

> 1 cup semisweet chocolate chips
> 3 egg whites
> 1 cup granulated sugar
> $\frac{1}{3}$ cup graham cracker crumbs
> $\frac{1}{2}$ teaspoon vanilla extract

Preheat the oven to 350°F. Lightly grease cookie sheets with butter.

Melt the chocolate in the top of a double boiler over barely simmering water. Remove from the hot water and set aside to cool for at least 5 minutes.

In a large mixing bowl, beat the egg whites until they hold stiff peaks. Add the sugar, $\frac{1}{4}$ cup at a time, continuing to beat until the mixture is smooth and glossy. Fold in the melted chocolate, the crumbs, and the vanilla.

Drop level teaspoonfuls, about $1\frac{1}{2}$ inches apart, onto the prepared cookie sheets. Bake for 15 minutes, or until the meringues are dry and the bottoms are lightly browned.

Oatmeal Lace Cookies

These thin, lacy cookies spread a lot while they bake, so be sure to leave plenty of room around them on the cookie sheet. One tablespoon of dough makes a large cookie. If you prefer smaller cookies, drop the dough from a teaspoon.

Makes about 35 large cookies

> 1 cup unsalted butter, at room temperature
> $\frac{1}{2}$ cup granulated sugar
> 1 cup firmly packed light brown sugar
> 2 eggs
> 2 teaspoons vanilla extract
> $\frac{1}{4}$ cup water
> 1 cup all-purpose flour
> $\frac{1}{4}$ teaspoon salt
> $\frac{1}{2}$ teaspoon baking soda
> 2 cups quick-cooking oatmeal
> $1\frac{1}{2}$ cups finely chopped walnuts

Preheat the oven to 350°F. Lightly grease cookie sheets with butter.

In a large mixing bowl, cream the butter and sugars together. Beat until the mixture is light and fluffy. Add the eggs and beat well. Beat in the vanilla and the water.

Sift the flour, salt, and baking soda together. Add the sifted ingredients to the batter, $\frac{1}{4}$ cup at a time, beating well after each addition. When the batter is smooth, stir in the oatmeal and the walnuts.

Drop the batter by rounded tablespoonfuls, about 4 inches apart, onto the prepared cookie sheets. Using a spatula, spread the mounds to a thickness of $\frac{1}{4}$ inch. Bake for 8 minutes, or until the cookies are golden brown.

Let the cookies cool on the cookie sheets for 2 minutes, then use a pancake turner to transfer them to wire racks to cool completely.

Pecan Clusters

A real confection, these cookies may be made with walnuts instead of pecans or with very coarsely chopped Brazil nuts.

Makes about 36 cookies

   1½ *ounces unsweetened chocolate*
   ¼ *cup unsalted butter, at room temperature*
   ½ *cup granulated sugar*
   1 *egg*
   1 *teaspoon vanilla extract*
   ½ *cup sifted all-purpose flour*
   ½ *teaspoon salt*
   ¼ *teaspoon baking powder*
   1½ *cups pecan pieces*
   1 *egg white*
   1 *teaspoon water*

Preheat the oven to 350°F. Lightly grease cookie sheets with butter.

In the top of a double boiler, melt the chocolate over barely simmering water. Remove from the hot water and set aside.

In a large mixing bowl, cream the butter and sugar together. Add the egg and the vanilla and beat until the mixture is light and fluffy. Add the melted chocolate and mix well.

Sift together the flour, salt, and baking powder. Fold the sifted ingredients into the batter. Fold in the nuts.

Drop heaping teaspoonfuls of batter, about 2 inches apart, onto the prepared cookie sheets.

In a small bowl, lightly beat the egg white with the water. Brush the cookies with the mixture.

Bake for 10 to 12 minutes, or until the cookies are firm.

Hermits

Full of raisins and nuts, these old-fashioned spice cookies improve with age. Store them in an airtight container for at least 2 weeks before serving.

Makes about 48 cookies

$\frac{3}{4}$ cup unsalted butter, at room temperature
$1\frac{1}{2}$ cups firmly packed dark brown sugar
2 eggs
$2\frac{1}{2}$ cups all-purpose flour
$\frac{1}{2}$ teaspoon baking soda
$\frac{1}{2}$ teaspoon salt
1 teaspoon ground nutmeg
$1\frac{1}{2}$ teaspoons ground cinnamon
1 cup coarsely chopped walnuts
1 cup dark raisins
1 cup golden raisins

Preheat the oven to 375°F. Lightly grease cookie sheets with butter.

In a large mixing bowl, cream the butter and sugar together. Add the eggs and beat until light and fluffy.

Sift together the flour, baking soda, salt, nutmeg, and cinnamon. Blend the sifted ingredients into the batter. Add the nuts and the raisins and mix well.

Drop teaspoonfuls of the batter, 2 inches apart, onto the prepared cookie sheets. Bake for about 10 minutes, or until the cookies are golden brown.

Walnut Rocks

Rocks are classic American cookies. They get their name from their shape, not their texture.

Makes about 50 cookies

$\frac{1}{2}$ cup unsalted butter, at room temperature
$\frac{1}{2}$ cup granulated sugar
2 eggs, separated
1 cup plus 2 tablespoons all-purpose flour
$\frac{1}{2}$ teaspoon ground cinnamon
$\frac{1}{2}$ teaspoon ground cloves
$\frac{1}{2}$ cup finely chopped walnuts
$\frac{3}{4}$ cup raisins
$\frac{1}{2}$ teaspoon baking soda
1 teaspoon boiling water

Preheat the oven to 350°F. Lightly flour cookie sheets.

In a large mixing bowl, cream the butter and sugar together. Beat in one egg yolk at a time.

Sift together the flour, cinnamon, and cloves. Add to the batter and mix well. Stir in the walnuts and the raisins. Dissolve the baking soda in the water, then stir it into the batter.

In a medium bowl, beat the egg whites until they hold stiff peaks. Fold them into the batter.

Drop teaspoonfuls of batter, about 2 inches apart, onto the prepared cookie sheets. Bake for 15 to 18 minutes, or until the outsides of the cookies are firm and the bottoms are golden brown.

Orange Drop Cookies

Speckled with grated orange rind, these simple cookies are very special.

Makes about 36 cookies

- $\frac{1}{2}$ *cup unsalted butter, at room temperature*
- $\frac{3}{4}$ *cup granulated sugar*
- *1 egg*
- $\frac{1}{2}$ *teaspoon baking soda*
- $1\frac{1}{2}$ *teaspoons baking powder*
- $1\frac{1}{2}$ *cups all-purpose flour*
- *1 cup buttermilk*
- *1 large navel orange*

Preheat the oven to 350°F.

In a large mixing bowl, cream the butter and sugar together, then beat until fluffy. Add the egg and beat well.

Sift together the baking soda, baking powder, and flour. Add the sifted ingredients to the batter, $\frac{1}{2}$ cup at a time, alternating with the buttermilk. Beat well after each addition.

Grate the rind and squeeze the juice of the orange. Add to the batter and mix well.

Drop by teaspoonfuls, about 2 inches apart, onto ungreased cookie sheets. Bake for 10 to 12 minutes, or until the bottoms of the cookies are lightly browned.

Coconut Cornflake Cookies

Easy to make, these chewy cookies are an unusual combination of simple ingredients.

Makes about 60 cookies

$\frac{3}{4}$ cup unsalted butter, at room temperature
2$\frac{1}{2}$ cups firmly packed dark brown sugar
3 eggs
2 teaspoons vanilla extract
1 cup flaked coconut
2 cups coarsely chopped walnuts
8$\frac{1}{2}$ cups cornflakes

Preheat the oven to 375°F. Lightly grease cookie sheets with butter.

In a large mixing bowl, cream the butter and sugar together. Add the eggs and the vanilla and beat until light and fluffy. Stir in the coconut and the walnuts and mix well. Add the cornflakes and mix gently but thoroughly.

Drop teaspoonfuls of batter, 2 inches apart, on the prepared cookie sheets. Bake for 8 to 10 minutes, or until the bottoms of the cookies are golden brown.

Let the cookies set on the cookie sheets for 5 minutes before transferring them to wire racks to cool completely.

Bar Cookies

Bar cookies are the easiest kind of cookie to make because they are baked all at once and then cut into squares, bars, or strips—but the ease of preparation does not make these cookies less varied or delicious.

For best results, always use the size of pan specified in the recipe. The pan may be made of aluminum, metal, or ovenproof glass. Use a rubber spatula to spread the batter evenly in the pan.

Cool bar cookies in the pan on a wire rack. Cut them into the size and shape you want using a sharp knife rinsed in cold water. Remove a bar from one corner first. The rest can then be removed easily. If you are going to ice the bars, always do so before cutting them.

Bar cookies are the easiest kind of cookie to store, too. Simply cover the bars in the baking pan with plastic wrap. Then cover the whole pan with foil and seal the edges tightly. Store in the refrigerator, or in the freezer if you are going to keep them for more than a week.

Holiday Layer Squares

Easy to make, these cookies are full of everyone's favorite ingredients. They are guaranteed to disappear quickly.

Makes 24 squares

> 4 tablespoons unsalted butter
> 1 cup graham cracker crumbs
> 1 cup flaked coconut
> 1 cup semisweet chocolate chips
> 1 cup finely chopped walnuts
> 1 cup sweetened condensed milk
> 1 cup candied cherries

Preheat the oven to 350°F.

Put the butter into an 8-inch square baking pan. Put the pan into the oven for a few minutes until the butter melts. Shake the pan so that the bottom and sides are coated with the melted butter.

Spread the graham cracker crumbs evenly over the bottom of the pan. Sprinkle a layer of coconut over the crumbs. Next make a layer of chocolate chips, then a layer of chopped nuts. Pour the condensed milk over the layers. Arrange the candied cherries on the top.

Bake for 30 minutes. Cool in the pan on a wire rack. When completely cool, cut into squares.

Fudge Brownies

This recipe makes moist, chewy brownies. If you prefer cakelike brownies, bake them for 5 minutes longer. Walnuts may, of course, be substituted for the pecans.

Makes about 20 brownies

  2 ounces unsweetened chocolate
  $\frac{1}{3}$ cup unsalted butter
  2 eggs
  1 cup granulated sugar
  1 teaspoon vanilla extract
  $\frac{2}{3}$ cup all-purpose flour
  $\frac{1}{4}$ teaspoon salt
  $\frac{1}{2}$ teaspoon baking powder
  $\frac{1}{2}$ cup coarsely chopped pecans

Preheat the oven to 350°F. Grease an 8-inch square baking pan with butter.

Combine the chocolate and the butter in the top of a double boiler. Cook over barely simmering water, stirring frequently, until the chocolate and butter are melted. Remove from the hot water and set aside.

In a large mixing bowl, beat the eggs until foamy. Add the sugar, $\frac{1}{4}$ cup at a time, beating well after each addition. Blend in the melted chocolate mixture and the vanilla.

Combine the flour, salt, and baking powder and add it to the batter. Mix well. Stir in the nuts.

Pour the batter into the prepared pan. Bake for 25 minutes. Cool the brownies in the pan on a wire rack, then cut into squares or bars.

Spicy Molasses Bars

Molasses is a traditional Christmas flavor, and in this recipe it is delightfully combined with spices, nuts, and fruit.

Makes about 24 bars

$\frac{1}{2}$ cup unsalted butter
1 cup all-purpose flour
$\frac{1}{4}$ teaspoon baking powder
$\frac{1}{8}$ teaspoon baking soda
$\frac{1}{2}$ teaspoon salt
$\frac{1}{2}$ teaspoon ground cinnamon
$\frac{1}{4}$ teaspoon ground ginger
$\frac{1}{4}$ teaspoon ground allspice
2 eggs
$\frac{2}{3}$ cup granulated sugar
$\frac{1}{4}$ cup dark molasses
$\frac{1}{2}$ cup diced candied cherries
$\frac{1}{2}$ cup finely chopped pecans
1 tablespoon grated orange rind

Preheat the oven to 350°F. Grease a 9-inch square baking pan.

In a small pan over very low heat, melt the butter. Set aside to cool.

Sift together the flour, baking powder, baking soda, salt, cinnamon, ginger, and allspice.

In a large mixing bowl, beat the eggs until light and foamy. Add the sugar and beat well. Beat in the molasses. Add the melted butter and mix well. Add the sifted ingredients and stir only until blended. Fold in the cherries, pecans, and grated orange rind.

Pour the batter into the prepared pan. Bake for 20 minutes, or until the top springs back when lightly touched. Cool in the pan on a wire rack, then cut into bars.

Pumpkin Shortbread Squares

These cookies have a shortbread base, a pumpkin and nut filling, and a crumb topping. They are delicious.

Makes 24 squares

> $\frac{3}{4}$ cup unsalted butter, at room temperature
> $\frac{2}{3}$ cup granulated sugar
> $\frac{3}{4}$ teaspoon vanilla extract
> $2\frac{1}{3}$ cups all-purpose flour
> $\frac{1}{2}$ teaspoon baking powder
> $\frac{1}{4}$ teaspoon salt
> 2 eggs
> 1 cup firmly packed dark brown sugar
> 1 cup canned pumpkin puree
> $\frac{1}{2}$ cup finely chopped pecans

Preheat the oven to 400°F. Lightly grease a 13 × 9-inch baking pan with butter.

In a mixing bowl, cream together $\frac{1}{2}$ cup of the butter, $\frac{1}{3}$ cup of the granulated sugar, and $\frac{1}{4}$ teaspoon of the vanilla. Add 1 cup of the flour, $\frac{1}{4}$ cup at a time, and mix well after each addition.

Press the dough into the bottom of the prepared pan. Bake for 5 minutes. Remove the pan from the oven and reduce the oven temperature to 350°F.

Sift together $\frac{1}{3}$ cup of the flour, the baking powder, and salt. In a large bowl, beat the eggs until foamy. Beat in the brown sugar, pumpkin, and the remaining $\frac{1}{2}$ teaspoon of vanilla. Stir in the sifted ingredients and the nuts. Spread the mixture over the partially baked shortbread.

In a medium bowl, combine the remaining 1 cup of flour and $\frac{1}{3}$ cup of granulated sugar. Using a pastry blender or two table knives, cut in the remaining $\frac{1}{4}$ cup of butter until the mixture resembles coarse crumbs. Sprinkle over the pumpkin layer.

Bake for 25 minutes. Cool in the pan on a wire rack. When completely cool, cut into squares.

Chocolate Chip Squares

Faster to make than traditional chocolate chip cookies, these bars will disappear just as quickly.

Makes about 24 squares

> 1 cup unsalted butter, at room temperature
> $\frac{3}{4}$ cup granulated sugar
> $\frac{3}{4}$ cup firmly packed dark brown sugar
> 1 teaspoon vanilla extract
> 2 eggs
> $1\frac{1}{4}$ cups all-purpose flour
> 1 teaspoon baking soda
> 1 teaspoon salt
> 2 cups semisweet chocolate chips
> 1 cup coarsely chopped walnuts

Preheat the oven to 350°F. Liberally grease a 13 × 9-inch baking pan with butter.

In a large mixing bowl, cream the butter and sugars together. Add the vanilla and the eggs and beat until light and fluffy.

Combine the flour, baking soda, and salt and sift it into the batter. Mix well. Stir in the chocolate chips and the walnuts.

Spread the batter in the prepared pan. Bake for 25 to 30 minutes, or until the top is golden brown. Cool in the pan on a wire rack, then cut into squares.

Hand-Shaped Cookies

The dough for all the cookies in this section is molded into balls. Some of them are then rolled in nuts, or sugar, or cinnamon; others are flattened. All of them are sure to become part of your Christmas-cookie repertoire.

Cookies that are shaped by hand must be made from dough that will not stick to your fingers while you are working with it. If the dough seems sticky, it is a good idea to chill it for several hours. For fast chilling, divide the dough in half, or even in quarters. Wrap each portion in plastic wrap or foil before putting it into the refrigerator. Work with only a small amount of the chilled dough at a time and keep the rest in the refrigerator until you are ready to use it.

Hand-shaped cookies that are not flattened should be baked until the edges are firm and the bottoms are a light golden brown. Use the tip of a table knife or a metal spatula to lift a cookie so you can peek at the underside.

Chocolate Teddy Bears

Everyone loves teddy bears, and these cookies will be no exception. If you are giving these teddy bears as gifts, tie a bow of bright, thin ribbon around each of their necks.

Makes 14 cookies

$\frac{2}{3}$ cup unsalted butter, at room temperature
1 cup granulated sugar
2 eggs
2 teaspoons vanilla extract
2$\frac{1}{2}$ cups all-purpose flour
$\frac{1}{2}$ cup cocoa
1 teaspoon baking soda
$\frac{1}{4}$ teaspoon salt
Raisins

In a large mixing bowl, cream the butter and sugar together, then beat until light and fluffy. Beat in the eggs. Add the vanilla and mix well. Combine the flour, cocoa, baking soda, and salt. Add to the batter, $\frac{1}{2}$ cup at a time, mixing well after each addition.

Gather the dough into two balls. Wrap each one in foil and chill in the refrigerator overnight.

Preheat the oven to 350°F.

Make the teddy bears one at a time. Shape dough into one 1-inch ball for the body, one $\frac{3}{4}$-inch ball for the head, six $\frac{1}{2}$-inch balls for the arms, legs, and ears, and five $\frac{1}{4}$-inch balls for the paws and nose.

On an ungreased cookie sheet, flatten the large ball so it is $\frac{1}{2}$ inch thick. Attach the head by overlapping it slightly on the body and then flatten it to $\frac{1}{2}$-inch thickness. Attach the legs, arms, and ears and flatten them slightly. Then place one of the tiny balls on the head for the nose. Arrange the remaining little balls on top of the ends of the arms and legs for paws. Gently press raisins into the dough to make eyes and a belly button.

Bake for 6 to 8 minutes, or until the edges of the cookies are firm. Cool for 1 minute on the cookie sheet, then transfer the cookies to wire racks to cool completely.

Walnut Cookie Balls

These cookies taste as good as they look. They add a festive touch to the holiday table—and they make a delicious gift.

Makes about 36 cookies

$\frac{1}{2}$ cup unsalted butter, at room temperature
$\frac{1}{3}$ cup honey
1 egg, separated
1 navel orange
$1\frac{1}{2}$ cups all-purpose flour
$\frac{1}{4}$ teaspoon baking soda
$\frac{1}{4}$ teaspoon salt
$\frac{1}{4}$ teaspoon ground nutmeg
$\frac{1}{2}$ teaspoon ground cinnamon
1 cup finely chopped walnuts
    Green and red candied cherries, halved

In a large mixing bowl, beat together the butter and the honey. Beat in the egg yolk. Grate the rind of the orange and add it to the batter. Squeeze 2 tablespoons of the orange juice and add it to the batter.

Sift together the flour, baking soda, salt, nutmeg, and cinnamon. Add the flour mixture to the batter, $\frac{1}{2}$ cup at a time, and blend well. Cover the bowl and refrigerate overnight.

Preheat the oven to 325°F. In a small bowl, beat the egg white until foamy. Spread the chopped walnuts on a plate.

Shape the dough into 36 balls. Dip each ball into the egg white, then roll it in the nuts.

Place the cookies 2 inches apart on ungreased cookie sheets. Lightly press half a candied cherry on top of each cookie. Bake for 15 minutes, or until the edges of the cookies are firm.

Peppernuts

These little treats improve with age. Store the peppernuts in an airtight container for several weeks to allow them to ripen. Before serving, they may be rolled in confectioners' sugar.

Makes about 110 cookies

3 cups all-purpose flour
1 teaspoon baking powder
$\frac{3}{4}$ teaspoon salt
$\frac{1}{2}$ teaspoon freshly ground black pepper
1 teaspoon ground cinnamon
$\frac{1}{2}$ teaspoon ground mace
1 teaspoon ground allspice
$\frac{1}{2}$ cup candied citron, finely chopped
$\frac{1}{4}$ cup candied orange peel, finely chopped
1 teaspoon grated lemon rind
3 eggs
$1\frac{1}{2}$ cups granulated sugar

Preheat the oven to 350°F. Lightly grease cookie sheets with butter.

Into a large mixing bowl, sift together the flour, baking powder, salt, black pepper, cinnamon, mace, and allspice. Add the citron, orange peel, and grated lemon rind and mix well.

In another bowl, combine the eggs and the sugar. Beat until thick and lemon colored. Add to the flour mixture and blend well. If necessary, knead the dough with your hands.

Pinch off small pieces of dough and shape into $\frac{3}{4}$-inch balls. Place them about 1 inch apart on the prepared cookie sheets. Bake for about 15 minutes, or until the bottoms of the cookies are lightly browned.

Spicy Chocolate Cookies

Black pepper may seem like an unusual ingredient for a cookie. In this recipe it intensifies the flavor of the chocolate and of the spices.

Makes about 36 cookies

$\frac{3}{4}$ cup unsalted butter, at room temperature
$\frac{3}{4}$ teaspoon freshly ground black pepper
$\frac{3}{4}$ teaspoon ground cinnamon
$\frac{1}{4}$ teaspoon ground cloves
1 cup granulated sugar
1 egg
$1\frac{1}{2}$ teaspoons vanilla extract
$1\frac{1}{4}$ cups all-purpose flour
$1\frac{1}{2}$ teaspoons baking powder
$\frac{1}{4}$ teaspoon salt
$\frac{3}{4}$ cup cocoa
Confectioners' sugar

Preheat the oven to 375°F. Lightly grease cookie sheets with butter.

In a large mixing bowl, cream the butter with the black pepper, cinnamon, cloves, and sugar. Beat in the egg and the vanilla.

Sift together the flour, baking powder, salt, and cocoa. Add the sifted ingredients, $\frac{1}{2}$ cup at a time, to the batter, mixing well after each addition.

Shape the dough into 1-inch balls. Place them 2 inches apart on the prepared cookie sheets. Dip the bottom of a glass into confectioners' sugar, then use it to flatten the balls to a thickness of $\frac{1}{4}$ inch.

Bake for 12 minutes, or until the edges of the cookies are lightly browned.

Pecan Spice Cookies

Chopped walnuts, hazelnuts, or even Brazil nuts may be substituted for the pecans in this recipe. The addition of $\frac{1}{2}$ cup of raisins also makes a good variation.

Makes about 72 cookies

  $\frac{3}{4}$ *cup unsalted butter, at room temperature*
  $\frac{1}{4}$ *teaspoon ground cloves*
  $\frac{1}{2}$ *teaspoon ground mace*
  $\frac{1}{2}$ *teaspoon ground ginger*
  $\frac{1}{2}$ *cup granulated sugar*
  1 *cup coarsely chopped pecans*
  2 *cups sifted all-purpose flour*
    Confectioners' sugar

Preheat the oven to 325°F.

In a large mixing bowl, cream the butter with the ground cloves, mace, and ginger. Gradually add the sugar and beat until the mixture is light and fluffy. Stir in the pecans. Add the flour, $\frac{1}{2}$ cup at a time, mixing well after each addition.

Shape the dough into 1-inch balls. Place them about 2 inches apart on ungreased cookie sheets. Bake for 20 minutes, or until the cookies are lightly browned around the edges.

Sift about $\frac{1}{2}$ cup of confectioners' sugar onto a large platter. While the cookies are warm, roll them in the sugar. Place them on wire racks to cool completely, then roll them in confectioners' sugar again.

Chocolate Chocolate Cookies

These rich chocolate cookies are marvelous at any time of the year, but they are particularly wonderful at Christmas because they are easy to make and keep extremely well in an airtight container.

Makes about 60 cookies

4 ounces German sweet chocolate
6 ounces unsweetened chocolate
1 cup unsalted butter, at room temperature
1 cup granulated sugar
1 cup firmly packed light brown sugar
2 eggs, lightly beaten
1 tablespoon vanilla extract
2 cups all-purpose flour
1 teaspoon baking soda
$\frac{1}{2}$ teaspoon salt

Combine the chocolate and the butter in the top of a double boiler set over barely simmering water. Cook, stirring frequently, until the chocolate and butter have melted. Remove from the hot water. Beat in the sugars, $\frac{1}{2}$ cup at a time. Then beat in the eggs and the vanilla. Continue to beat until the mixture is smooth, then pour it into a large mixing bowl.

Sift together the flour, baking soda, and salt. Gradually add the sifted ingredients to the chocolate mixture, stirring only until the flour is absorbed.

Cover the bowl and put it into the refrigerator for about 1 hour.

Preheat the oven to 375°F. Lightly grease cookie sheets with butter.

Form the dough into 1-inch balls. Place the balls about 2 inches apart on the prepared cookie sheets. Bake for 10 minutes.

Let the cookies cool on the cookie sheets for about 3 minutes before transferring them to wire racks to cool completely.

Date Walnut Cookies

Dates and walnuts are an unbeatable combination and these cookies are easy to make, too.

Makes about 60 cookies

$\frac{2}{3}$ cup unsalted butter, at room temperature
1 cup granulated sugar
1 cup firmly packed dark brown sugar
2 teaspoons vanilla extract
2 eggs
1 cup coarsely chopped pitted dates
1 cup coarsely chopped walnuts
3 cups sifted all-purpose flour
1 teaspoon baking soda
$\frac{1}{2}$ teaspoon salt
Confectioners' sugar

Preheat the oven to 375°F. Lightly grease cookie sheets with butter.

In a large mixing bowl, cream the butter and sugars together. Add the vanilla and beat until light and fluffy. Beat in the eggs. Add the dates and the nuts and mix well.

Sift together the flour, baking soda, and salt. Add to the batter, $\frac{1}{2}$ cup at a time, mixing well after each addition.

Shape tablespoonfuls of dough into balls. Place the balls about 3 inches apart on the prepared cookie sheets. Dip the bottom of a glass into confectioners' sugar, then use it to flatten the cookies.

Bake for 10 to 12 minutes, or until the edges of the cookies are lightly browned.

Chocolate Crackles

The tops of these chewy cookies are puffy and crackled. Be sure not to overbake them.

Makes about 50 cookies

  4 ounces unsweetened chocolate
  1 teaspoon vanilla extract
  $\frac{1}{2}$ cup unsalted butter, at room temperature
  1$\frac{3}{4}$ cups granulated sugar
  3 eggs
  2 cups plus 2 tablespoons all-purpose flour
  2 teaspoons baking powder
  $\frac{1}{4}$ teaspoon salt
  $\frac{1}{2}$ cup confectioners' sugar

In the top of a double boiler, melt the chocolate over barely simmering water. Remove from the hot water and stir in the vanilla. Set aside.

In a large mixing bowl, cream the butter and sugar together, then beat until fluffy. Add the eggs and beat well. Add the chocolate mixture and beat until well blended.

Combine the flour, baking powder, and salt. Add to the batter, $\frac{1}{2}$ cup at a time, mixing after each addition only enough to blend the ingredients. Cover the bowl and chill the dough in the refrigerator for 2 hours.

Preheat the oven to 350°F. Lightly grease cookie sheets with butter. Spread the confectioners' sugar on a plate.

Shape heaping teaspoonfuls of dough into balls. Roll the balls in the confectioners' sugar then place them 1$\frac{1}{2}$ inches apart on the prepared cookie sheets.

Bake for 10 to 12 minutes, or until the tops of the cookies are puffed and crackled.

Sandies

These buttery, nutty cookies are traditional Christmas favorites.

Makes about 48 cookies

> 1 cup unsalted butter, at room temperature
> $\frac{1}{3}$ cup granulated sugar
> 2 teaspoons water
> 2 teaspoons vanilla extract
> $2\frac{1}{4}$ cups all-purpose flour
> 1 cup finely chopped pecans
> $\frac{1}{4}$ cup confectioners' sugar

Preheat the oven to 325°F.

In a large mixing bowl, cream the butter and sugar together. Beat until light and fluffy. Beat in the water and the vanilla. Blend in the flour, $\frac{1}{2}$ cup at a time. Add the pecans and mix well.

Shape the dough into 1-inch balls. Place them about $1\frac{1}{2}$ inches apart on ungreased cookie sheets.

Bake for 20 minutes, or until the edges of the cookies are firm and the bottoms are lightly browned. Transfer the cookies to wire racks to cool.

Sift the confectioners' sugar onto a large plate. When the cookies are completely cool, roll each one in the sugar.

Gingersnaps

Crisp and spicy, these cookies are a wonderful addition to the Christmas cookie jar.

Makes about 48 cookies

$2\frac{1}{2}$ cups all-purpose flour
2 teaspoons baking soda
1 teaspoon ground ginger
1 teaspoon ground cinnamon
$\frac{1}{2}$ teaspoon ground cloves
$\frac{1}{4}$ teaspoon salt
1 cup firmly packed dark brown sugar
$\frac{3}{4}$ cup corn oil
$\frac{1}{4}$ cup molasses
1 egg

Preheat the oven to 375°F.

Sift together the flour, baking soda, ginger, cinnamon, cloves, and salt.

In a large mixing bowl, combine the sugar, oil, molasses, and egg. Beat well. Add the flour mixture, $\frac{1}{2}$ cup at a time, beating well after each addition. Continue to beat until the dough is smooth.

Shape the dough into 1-inch balls. Place the balls 2 inches apart on ungreased cookie sheets.

Bake for 10 minutes, or until the edges of the cookies are firm.

Special Cookies

Spritz cookies made with a cookie press, tiny pies, miniature fruitcakes, cookies made from dough that must be refrigerated overnight—these cookies are a little more difficult or time-consuming to make—but they are all well worth the additional time and effort.

Be sure to read each recipe through before beginning to bake, and then follow it exactly.

Spritz Cookies

These cookies require a cookie press, a piece of equipment no dedicated cookie baker should be without. Use whichever decorative blades you prefer.

Makes about 36 cookies

1 cup unsalted butter, at room temperature
$\frac{2}{3}$ cup granulated sugar
1 egg
1 teaspoon vanilla extract
$\frac{1}{2}$ teaspoon grated lemon rind
2$\frac{1}{4}$ cups all-purpose flour
$\frac{1}{4}$ teaspoon salt
  Colored sugar

Preheat the oven to 375°F.

In a large mixing bowl, cream the butter and sugar together, then beat until light and fluffy. Beat in the egg, then the vanilla. Add the grated lemon rind and mix well.

Sift the flour and salt together. Add it to the batter, $\frac{1}{2}$ cup at a time, mixing well after each addition.

Using one-quarter of the dough at a time, place it in a cookie press fitted with a decorative blade. Hold the press upright and force the dough onto ungreased cookie sheets, leaving about 1$\frac{1}{2}$ inches between cookies. Sprinkle the cookies with colored sugar.

Bake for about 10 minutes, or until the cookies are golden.

Chocolate Spritz Ribbons

To make these rich cookies, a cookie press is required. And if you prefer rosettes to ribbons, it is easy to change the blade.

Makes about 50 cookies

2 ounces unsweetened chocolate
1 cup unsalted butter, at room temperature
$\frac{2}{3}$ cup granulated sugar
3 egg yolks
1 teaspoon vanilla extract
$\frac{1}{4}$ cup ground almonds
$2\frac{1}{2}$ cups all-purpose flour, sifted

Preheat the oven to 400°F.

In the top of a double boiler, melt the chocolate over barely simmering water. Remove from the hot water and set aside.

In a large mixing bowl, cream the butter and sugar together. Add the egg yolks and the vanilla and beat until light. Blend in the melted chocolate.

Combine the almonds and the flour. Add to the batter, $\frac{1}{2}$ cup at a time, blending well after each addition.

Using one-quarter of the dough at a time, place it in a cookie press fitted with a decorative blade. Holding the press upright, force the dough onto ungreased cookie sheets in ribbons about 2 inches long and $1\frac{1}{2}$ inches apart.

Bake for 7 to 10 minutes, or until the cookies are set.

Pecan Pie Cookies

These miniature pecan pies are made in $1\frac{3}{4}$-inch mini muffin tins. They are unusual—a very special holiday treat.

Makes about 60 cookies

    6 *ounce package cream cheese*
    1 *cup unsalted butter, at room temperature*
    2 *cups sifted all-purpose flour*

Filling
    4 *tablespoons unsalted butter, at room temperature*
    $1\frac{1}{2}$ *cups firmly packed dark brown sugar*
    2 *eggs*
    2 *teaspoons vanilla extract*
    $1\frac{3}{4}$ *cups finely chopped pecans*

Preheat the oven to 325°F.

In a large mixing bowl, cream together the cream cheese and the butter, then beat until fluffy. Blend in the flour, $\frac{1}{2}$ cup at a time, and mix to a smooth dough.

Put a small ball of dough into each muffin tin, then, using a thumb, press it into the tin so that it thinly lines the bottom and side, like piecrust. Set aside.

To make the filling, in a large mixing bowl, cream together the butter and the sugar. Add the eggs and beat well. Beat in the vanilla. Stir in the nuts. Fill the lined muffin tins half full. The filling will rise as it bakes.

Bake for 25 minutes, or until the top of the filling is lightly browned. Cool on wire racks, then remove the little pies from the tins, using the tip of a table knife to flip each one out.

60

Christmas Fantasy Cookies

These colored cookies are unusually pretty. The dough must be refrigerated overnight before baking.

Makes about 60 cookies

> 1 cup unsalted butter, at room temperature
> 1 cup sifted confectioners' sugar
> 1 teaspoon vanilla extract
> 1 tablespoon corn syrup
> 2½ cups all-purpose flour
> 1 teaspoon salt
> 2 tablespoons milk
>   Red and green food coloring

In a large mixing bowl, cream together the butter and sugar. Beat in the vanilla and the corn syrup.

Sift together the flour and the salt. Add the sifted ingredients to the batter, ½ cup at a time, blending well after each addition. Add the milk, a little at a time, but only as much as necessary to make a smooth, but stiff, dough.

Divide the dough into three parts. Add 6 drops of green food coloring to one part and 6 drops of red food coloring to the second part. Leave the third part uncolored. Blend the food coloring into the dough thoroughly. It will probably be necessary to knead it with your hands.

Mix the three pieces of dough together carefully so that each color remains distinct. The dough should have a marbled effect. Shape the dough into a roll about 2 inches in diameter. Wrap in foil and chill overnight in the refrigerator.

Preheat the oven to 375°F.

Using a very sharp knife, cut the dough into slices ⅛ inch thick. Place the cookies about ½ inch apart on ungreased cookie sheets.

Bake for 8 to 10 minutes. Do not let the cookies brown.

Miniature Fruitcakes

Great for holiday gift giving, these tiny fruitcakes are more confections than cookies. They will improve with age if they are stored for several weeks in airtight containers. Apple juice may be substituted for the brandy.

Makes 60 tiny fruitcakes

$1\frac{1}{2}$ cups diced candied fruit
1 cup raisins
$\frac{1}{2}$ cup currants
1 cup brandy
$\frac{1}{3}$ cup unsalted butter, at room temperature
$\frac{3}{4}$ cup firmly packed dark brown sugar
1 egg
1 cup all-purpose flour
$\frac{1}{2}$ teaspoon baking soda
$\frac{1}{2}$ teaspoon salt
$\frac{1}{2}$ teaspoon ground allspice
$\frac{1}{2}$ teaspoon ground cinnamon
$\frac{1}{4}$ teaspoon ground nutmeg
1 cup finely chopped walnuts
    Red and green candied cherries

In a medium bowl, combine the candied fruit, raisins, and currants. Add $\frac{1}{2}$ cup of the brandy and mix well. Cover the bowl and set aside overnight to let the fruit marinate in the brandy.

Preheat the oven to 300°F. Line $1\frac{3}{4}$-inch mini muffin tins with foil baking cups.

In a large mixing bowl, cream the butter and sugar together. Beat until fluffy. Beat in the egg.

Sift together the flour, baking soda, salt, allspice, cinnamon, and nutmeg. Add to the batter and mix until well blended. Add the walnuts and marinated fruit and mix well.

Spoon the batter into the baking cups, filling them only three-quarters full. Press a candied cherry into the center of each one.

Bake for 30 minutes. Transfer the baking cups to wire racks and brush the top of each fruitcake with some of the reserved brandy.

Christmas Candy

Christmas Candy
Contents

Introduction   69
Making the Best Candy   70
Storing Candy   73
Packaging Candy and Other Confections   74

Chocolate Delights   75
Rocky Road   76
Chocolate Nut Truffles   77
Chocolate Rum Truffles   78
Milk Chocolate Truffles   79
Double Chocolate Delights   80
Chocolate Bourbon Balls   80
Chocolate Coconut Cups   81
Chocolate Walnut Drops   82

Divinity and Other Divine Candies   83
Divinity Kisses   84
Chocolate Divinity   85
Divinity Squares   86
Coconut Cherry Patties   87
Maple Pecan Candy   88
Pralines   89
Peppermint Creams   90

Fudge Favorites 91
Old-Fashioned Chocolate Fudge 92
Penuche 93
Fruit Fudge 94
Banana Walnut Fudge 95
Creamy Chocolate Pecan Fudge 96
Butterscotch Walnut Fudge 97
Mocha Fudge Slices 98

Christmas Confections 99
Popcorn Balls 100
Almond Pecan Popcorn 101
Walnut Treats 102
Fruit Chews 103
Walnut Date Slices 104
Taffy Apples 105
Candied Orange Peel 106
Candied Kumquats 107

Introduction

The marvelous confections of Christmas are surprisingly easy to make right in your own kitchen. In this new collection of recipes, you'll find a variety of scrumptious treats—luscious pecan pralines and creamy fudge, light fluffy divinity and nut-studded popcorn, bright candied fruit and crunchy spiced nuts, sweet taffy apples and sumptuous chocolate truffles.

Making candy is very satisfying, and homemade candy is especially delicious. Candy keeps well and travels well. Packed in a decorative tin, a pretty box, a beribboned jar, or, perhaps, a cut-glass dish, it makes a special gift, even for people who live far away. Homemade candy can be tucked into Christmas stockings. It is wonderful to nibble on while trimming the tree. And nothing is more fun during the holidays than making old-fashioned popcorn balls.

All of these recipes are easy-to-follow. (And, other than an inexpensive candy thermometer, no special equipment is required.) You can whip up a batch of old favorites like peppermint creams, chocolate truffles, pralines, rocky road, and butterscotch walnut fudge. Or try making such delights as candied kumquats and candied orange peel, fruit chews, walnut date slices, coconut cherry patties, and taffy apples. For entertaining and for special gifts, homemade candy is a welcome treat at any season of the year. You will enjoy rave reviews from your family and friends, for there is a recipe here to please every sweet tooth.

Making the Best Candy

Candy is not difficult to make. Some of the recipes in this book require little or no cooking. Others need only careful timing and adequate beating. For some types of candy, however, special care is necessary. Follow these basic instructions and you can become a successful and versatile candymaker.

🌲 Always read a recipe through from beginning to end before starting to cook.

🌲 Always use the best-quality, freshest ingredients available.

🌲 Measure ingredients accurately, using standard measuring spoons for small amounts, a fluid measuring cup for liquids, and graduated measuring cups for dry ingredients.

🌲 Follow recipes carefully. Use only the ingredients specified and add them in the order and by the method given.

🌲 To prevent sugaring, carefully follow directions about stirring and about covering the pan.

🌲 Use moderate or low heat, according to instructions in the recipe, so the syrup does not reach the boiling point too quickly.

🌲 Always use a saucepan large enough to allow space for the candy to bubble up when boiling. A 2-quart pan is large enough in most cases, but sometimes a 3-quart or even a 4-quart pan is preferable. A pan in which candy is made should be of heavy-gauge metal, which holds heat evenly and will prevent sticking.

🌲 Candymaking involves a lot of stirring and beating. Although an electric mixer may be used in some stages of preparation, such as beating egg whites for divinity, for most candy mixtures a spoon is best. A long-handled wooden spoon is preferable, since it will never get too hot to handle.

🌲 A candy thermometer that clips onto the side of the pan is almost a necessity for successful candymaking, since it is critical that the candy be removed from the heat at the moment it reaches the proper temperature. It is best to use a clearly marked, easy-to-read thermometer with a mercury ball that is set low enough to measure the temperature of the boiling syrup, but does not touch the bottom of the pan.

To use a candy thermometer, be sure it is at room temperature before putting it into the hot syrup. Lower the thermometer gradually into the candy mixture *after* the sugar is dissolved and the syrup has begun to boil.

🌲 The cold-water test is an alternative to a candy thermometer. Many cooks still rely upon this test, although it is not as accurate as a candy thermometer. (All the recipes in this book specify a temperature reading as well as the cold-water test results, such as hard ball or soft ball.)

Temperature Tests for Candy

Temperature of Syrup	Test	Description of Syrup When Dropped Into Very Cold Water
234° to 240°F	Soft ball	Forms a soft ball that flattens on removal from water
244° to 248°F	Firm ball	Forms a firm ball that does not flatten on removal from water
250° to 266°F	Hard ball	Forms a hard ball that, on removal from water, remains hard enough to hold its shape, yet is pliable
270° to 290°F	Soft crack	Separates into threads that are hard, but not brittle, when removed from water
300° to 310°F	Hard crack	Separates into threads that are hard and very brittle

To water-test, use very cold, but not ice, water. Use a clean cup, spoon, and fresh water for each test. Remove the pan from the heat and drop a little of the hot mixture into the water. Use your fingers to gather the drops into a ball and feel its consistency. If the candy is not yet ready, immediately return the pan to the heat.

🌲 Avoid making candy on damp or rainy days. High humidity is the candymaker's enemy. If for any reason you cannot postpone a candymaking session, cook the candy 1 or 2 degrees higher on the thermometer than indicated in the recipe.

🌲 Altitude also affects candymaking. Temperatures given in recipes in this book are for sea level. At high altitudes the candy must be cooked about 2 degrees higher.

🌲 Be patient and always allow sufficient time. Most candy does take time to make, and there is no way to rush the cooking without disaster.

Storing Candy

One of the nicest things about homemade candy is that it can be eaten when it is at its freshest. In addition, it contains no chemicals, artificial flavoring, or preservatives, although the lack of preservatives does limit its storage capabilities. Most homemade candy, however, will keep well for several weeks if it is stored properly. (The exception is divinity, which gets stale quickly and should be eaten within two days of preparation.) Here are some rules for storing candy successfully.

🌲 Sticky and chewy candies, like taffy, nougat, and caramels, and hard candies, like butterscotch, should be individually wrapped in waxed paper, plastic wrap, or foil.

🌲 All candy keeps best in an airtight container in a cool, dry place. Some chocolate candies, like truffles, are best stored in the refrigerator.

🌲 Do not store brittle candies in the same container with soft, creamy candies. The moisture from the soft candies may make the hard candies sticky.

🌲 Candy freezes well. Place the candy, individually wrapped if appropriate, in a cardboard box or plastic container. Overwrap the container with freezer paper or foil. To thaw the candy, let it stand for several hours, or overnight, and come to room temperature before opening the container. This will prevent moisture from collecting on the candies because of the temperature change.

Packaging Candy and Other Confections

Homemade confections are a wonderful present for a neighbor, a host or hostess, or a friend. You can make the packaging itself part of the gift by using decorative tins, boxes, and gift bags. Or create your own unique container by covering a plain box or tin with fabric or paper. Try sponge-painting or stenciling. Let your imagination run free.

To pack your confections in a round container, first line it with several layers of white doilies. Cut several rounds of waxed paper, a little smaller than the circumference of the box. Arrange the candy on the doilies in the box, then place several thicknesses of waxed paper, then a doily, on top. Tie a ribbon crosswise around the closed box. This would be a nice way to present pralines or walnut treats.

Fudge squares are best packed in a square box. Each square can be put into a foil or paper candy cup. Use square doilies to line the box and several thicknesses of waxed paper between layers of the candy.

Candied orange peel or kumquats look attractive in a wide-mouthed glass jar with a well-fitting lid. Wrap the jar using several layers of colored tissue paper. Gather the tissue paper at the top with curling ribbon.

A shiny, decorative tin pail is an excellent container for popcorn balls or almond pecan popcorn. Pack the popcorn in a large plastic bag before putting it into the pail. Then put the lid on the pail, seal it with transparent tape, and tie a big, bright bow on top.

When packaging chocolate candies, such as truffles, bourbon balls, or chocolate walnut drops, put each piece into a foil or paper candy cup before putting it into a gift box.

Chocolate bourbon balls, rocky road, chocolate walnut drops, a variety of truffles—these chocolate treats are exceptionally easy to make. Many of them need no cooking, and none of them requires a candy thermometer or cold-water test. Be sure, however, to use the best-quality chocolate available and when melting the chocolate to do so in the top of a double boiler over barely simmering water.

Rocky Road

Chocolate, marshmallows, nuts, and coconut combine to make this the richest and best-ever rocky road. If you are going to include this candy in a gift box, put each square in a foil candy cup.

> 2 *cups semisweet chocolate chips*
> 2¼ *cups miniature marshmallows*
> ¼ *cup flaked coconut*
> ½ *cup coarsely chopped walnuts*

Line an 8-inch square pan with foil. Grease the foil with butter.

In the top of a double boiler, melt the chocolate over barely simmering water, stirring constantly.

Remove from the hot water and stir in the marshmallows, coconut, and walnuts.

Pour the candy into the prepared pan and, using a spatula, spread it into an even layer. Chill in the refrigerator for about 3 hours, or until the candy is firm.

Remove the candy from the pan. Peel off the foil and, using a sharp knife, cut the candy into 1-inch squares.

Chocolate Nut Truffles

The secret of successful truffles is the quality of the chocolate. Always use the best chocolate available. Truffles should be stored in a covered container in the refrigerator. They will keep for about two weeks. Serve them at room temperature.

8 ounces semisweet chocolate
6 tablespoons unsalted butter
$\frac{1}{2}$ cup heavy cream
1 teaspoon vanilla extract
$\frac{1}{2}$ cup finely chopped almonds

In the top of a double boiler, melt the chocolate and the butter over barely simmering water, stirring constantly. Remove from the hot water and set aside.

In a small, heavy saucepan, bring the cream just to the boil. Remove from the heat and pour the cream into the chocolate mixture. Mix well. Add the vanilla and stir until the mixture is smooth. Pour into a shallow bowl and set aside to cool, stirring occasionally.

Cover the bowl and chill in the refrigerator for about 4 hours, or until the mixture is firm, but not solid.

Spread the chopped nuts on a plate. Scoop up the chocolate mixture with a teaspoon and shape it into rough balls. Roll the balls in the nuts.

Chocolate Rum Truffles

These truffles are sinfully rich—and very satisfying. Grand Marnier or Kahlúa may be substituted for the rum. Store the truffles, covered, in the refrigerator. Let them stand at room temperature for about 30 minutes before serving.

 2 *tablespoons heavy cream*
 2 *tablespoons dark rum*
 6 *ounces dark sweet chocolate, coarsely chopped*
 4 *tablespoons unsalted butter, cut into chunks*
 $\frac{1}{2}$ *cup unsweetened cocoa powder*

In a small, heavy pan, bring the cream just to a boil. Remove the pan from the heat and stir in the rum and the chocolate. Cook over very low heat, stirring constantly, until the chocolate melts.

Remove the pan from the heat and quickly mix the butter into the chocolate mixture. When the butter has melted and the mixture is smooth, pour it into a shallow bowl and set aside to cool. Cover the bowl and chill in the refrigerator for about 2 hours, or until the mixture is firm enough to handle.

Sift the cocoa onto a large plate. Scoop up the chocolate mixture with a teaspoon and shape it into rough balls. Roll each ball in the cocoa.

Milk Chocolate Truffles

Lightly spiced with cinnamon, these milk chocolate truffles are sweet, rich, and creamy. Store them covered in the refrigerator, but serve them at room temperature.

6 ounces milk chocolate
$\frac{1}{2}$ teaspoon ground cinnamon
1$\frac{1}{2}$ teaspoons unsalted butter, at room temperature
$\frac{1}{2}$ cup less 1 teaspoon sweetened condensed milk
$\frac{1}{2}$ teaspoon vanilla extract
$\frac{1}{2}$ cup chocolate sprinkles

In the top of a double boiler, melt the chocolate over barely simmering water, stirring constantly.

Remove from the hot water and stir in the cinnamon and the butter. When the butter is melted and the mixture is smooth, add the condensed milk and the vanilla. Stir until well blended.

Pour the mixture into a shallow bowl. Cover the bowl and chill in the refrigerator for 3 hours, or until the mixture is firm enough to handle.

Spread the chocolate sprinkles on a large plate. Scoop up the chocolate mixture with a teaspoon and shape it into balls. Roll each ball in the chocolate sprinkles.

Double Chocolate Delights

This luscious candy is extremely easy to make. It should be stored in a covered container in the refrigerator.

8 *ounces unsweetened chocolate*
4 *ounces German's sweet chocolate*
15 *ounce can sweetened condensed milk*
1 *cup finely chopped pecans*

In the top of a double boiler, melt the chocolates over barely simmering water, stirring constantly. Add the condensed milk and stir until well blended. Remove from the hot water. Pour the mixture into a shallow bowl and set aside to cool.

Cover the bowl and chill in the refrigerator for 1 hour, or until the mixture is firm enough to handle.

Spread the chopped nuts on a large plate. Scoop up the chocolate mixture with a teaspoon and shape it into balls. Roll each ball in the nuts.

Chocolate Bourbon Balls

These delicious candies require no cooking and will keep well in an airtight container in a cool place. Whiskey, rum, or your favorite liquor may be substituted for the bourbon.

1 *cup chocolate-wafer cookie crumbs*
2 *cups coarsely chopped pecans*
1 *cup confectioners' sugar*
$1\frac{1}{2}$ *tablespoons light corn syrup*
$\frac{1}{4}$ *cup bourbon*

In a blender or food processor, coarsely grind the cookie

crumbs with 1 cup of the pecans. Transfer to a large mixing bowl. Add the sugar, corn syrup, and bourbon and mix thoroughly.

Shape the mixture into 1-inch balls.

Spread the remaining 1 cup of pecans on a plate. Roll the balls in the nuts.

Chocolate Coconut Cups

These elegant candies couldn't be easier to make. After they are firm, they may be stored in an airtight container in a cool, dry place.

8 ounces bittersweet chocolate
1⅓ cups flaked coconut

Put 25 foil candy cups on a cookie sheet.

In the top of a double boiler, melt the chocolate over barely simmering water, stirring constantly.

Remove from the hot water and add the coconut. Mix lightly until the coconut is completely coated with the chocolate.

Drop a teaspoonful of the mixture into each foil cup. Chill in the refrigerator until firm.

Chocolate Walnut Drops

These delicious candies are easy to make. They should be stored in an airtight container in a cool, dry place.

1 cup firmly packed dark brown sugar
$\frac{1}{3}$ cup evaporated milk
2 tablespoons light corn syrup
1 cup semisweet chocolate chips
$\frac{1}{2}$ cup finely chopped walnuts
1 teaspoon vanilla extract
Walnut halves

Line a cookie sheet with waxed paper.

In a heavy saucepan, combine the sugar, milk, and corn syrup. Cook over moderate heat, stirring constantly, until the sugar is dissolved and the mixture comes to a boil. Boil, stirring constantly, for 2 minutes.

Remove the pan from the heat. Add the chocolate chips, chopped walnuts, and vanilla and stir until the chocolate is melted and the mixture is slightly thickened.

Drop the candy by rounded teaspoonfuls onto the prepared cookie sheet. Press a walnut half on top of each mound.

Chill in the refrigerator for 30 minutes, or until the candies are firm.

Christmas Wishes

Divinity and Other Divine Candies

Light-as-air divinity, pecan-studded pralines, and classic pepper-mint creams are among the delights included here. None of these candies is difficult to make. Some don't require a candy thermometer or cold-water testing. Most of them are drop candies. When dropping these or any candies from a spoon, be sure to work quickly or the mixture may harden in the bowl. Do not attempt to make any of these candies on a humid or rainy day, because, even if the recipes are followed to the letter, the candy will not set properly.

Divinity Kisses

Light and sweet, divinity is a distant cousin of meringue. To make coconut divinity, substitute $\frac{3}{4}$ cup of flaked coconut for the walnuts and omit the cherries.

   2$\frac{1}{2}$ cups granulated sugar
   $\frac{1}{2}$ cup light corn syrup
   $\frac{1}{2}$ cup water
   $\frac{1}{4}$ teaspoon salt
   2 large egg whites, at room temperature
   1 teaspoon vanilla extract
   $\frac{1}{2}$ cup coarsely chopped walnuts
      Red and green candied cherries, halved

Spread a large piece of waxed paper on a work surface.

In a large, heavy saucepan, combine the sugar, corn syrup, water, and salt. Cook over moderate heat, stirring constantly, until the sugar is dissolved. Cover the pan and continue to cook over moderate heat until the mixture comes to a boil, 2 to 3 minutes. Remove the lid and continue cooking, without stirring, until the syrup reaches the hard-ball stage (265°F on a candy thermometer).

While the syrup is cooking, in a large mixing bowl beat the egg whites until stiff peaks form.

Pour the hot syrup into the egg whites in a fine stream, beating constantly and at high speed with an electric mixer. When the mixture becomes thick and heavy, it will be necessary to use a wooden spoon to beat it. Add the vanilla and continue beating until the candy just holds its shape when dropped from the spoon. Quickly stir in the nuts.

Drop the candy by rounded teaspoonfuls onto the waxed paper. Press a candied cherry half into each kiss.

Chocolate Divinity

No candy is as divine as divinity, and for the chocoholic nothing beats chocolate divinity.

3 tablespoons unsalted butter
$\frac{1}{2}$ cup unsweetened cocoa powder
$2\frac{1}{2}$ cups granulated sugar
$\frac{1}{2}$ cup light corn syrup
$\frac{1}{3}$ cup water
$\frac{1}{4}$ teaspoon salt
2 large egg whites
1 teaspoon vanilla extract
$\frac{3}{4}$ cup finely chopped walnuts

Spread a large piece of waxed paper on a work surface.

In the top of a double boiler, melt the butter over hot, not boiling, water. Add the cocoa and stir until smooth. Remove from the hot water and set aside.

In a large, heavy saucepan, combine the sugar, corn syrup, water, and salt. Cook over moderate heat, stirring constantly, until the sugar is dissolved. Cover the pan and continue to cook over moderate heat, until the mixture comes to a boil, 2 to 3 minutes. Remove the lid and continue cooking without stirring, until the syrup reaches the hard-ball stage (265°F on a candy thermometer).

While the syrup is cooking, in a large mixing bowl beat the egg whites until stiff peaks form.

Pour the hot syrup into the egg whites in a fine stream, beating constantly and at high speed with an electric mixer. When the mixture becomes thick and heavy, it will be necessary to use a wooden spoon to beat it. Add the vanilla and continue beating until the candy just holds its shape when dropped from the spoon. Quickly blend in the cocoa mixture, then the nuts.

Drop the candy by teaspoonfuls onto the waxed paper.

Divinity Squares

These divinity squares are topped with chocolate and chopped walnuts—and they are very special.

> 2½ cups granulated sugar
> ½ cup light corn syrup
> ½ cup water
> ¼ teaspoon salt
> 2 large egg whites, at room temperature
> 1 teaspoon vanilla extract
> 2 ounces semisweet chocolate
> ¾ cup finely chopped walnuts

Grease an 8-inch square pan with butter.

In a large, heavy saucepan, combine the sugar, corn syrup, water, and salt. Cook over moderate heat, stirring constantly, until the sugar is dissolved. Cover the pan and continue to cook over moderate heat until the mixture comes to a boil, 2 to 3 minutes. Remove the lid and continue cooking, without stirring, until the mixture reaches the hard-ball stage (265°F on a candy thermometer).

While the syrup is cooking, in a large mixing bowl beat the egg whites until stiff peaks form.

Pour the hot syrup into the egg whites in a fine stream, beating constantly and at high speed with an electric mixer. When the mixture becomes thick and heavy it will be necessary to use a wooden spoon to beat it. Add the vanilla and continue beating until the candy just holds its shape when dropped from the spoon.

Spoon the divinity into the prepared pan. Using a rubber spatula, smooth it into an even layer.

In the top of a double boiler, melt the chocolate over barely simmering water, stirring constantly. Remove from the hot water and set aside to cool.

Pour the cooled melted chocolate over the divinity and spread in an even layer with a clean rubber spatula. Sprinkle the chopped nuts over the chocolate.

When the candy has cooled completely, use a sharp knife to cut it into squares.

Coconut Cherry Patties

Top these creamy patties with red and green candied cherry halves for a festive look. If you prefer, you can substitute pecan or walnut halves.

2 cups granulated sugar
½ cup milk
1½ cups flaked coconut
1 teaspoon vanilla extract
   Red and green candied cherries, halved

Spread a large sheet of waxed paper on a work surface.

In a heavy saucepan combine the sugar and the milk. Cook over high heat, stirring constantly, until the sugar is dissolved. Reduce the heat to moderate and cook, stirring constantly, until the mixture reaches the soft-ball stage (238°F on a candy thermometer).

Remove the pan from the heat and stir in the coconut and the vanilla.

Drop the candy by teaspoonfuls, about 2 inches apart, onto the waxed paper. With a spatula flatten each mound. Place half a candied cherry in the center of each patty.

Maple Pecan Candy

This luscious, creamy candy takes about 20 minutes to make—
and it's so easy you don't even need a candy thermometer.

> 4 *cups pure maple syrup*
> 1 *cup heavy cream*
> $\frac{1}{4}$ *cup unsalted butter*
> 1 *cup coarsely chopped pecans*
> 1 *teaspoon lemon extract*

Liberally grease an 8-inch square pan with butter.

In a heavy saucepan, combine the maple syrup, cream, and
butter. Cook over moderate heat, stirring constantly, until the
mixture comes to a boil. Continue cooking for 9 minutes, stirring frequently.

Remove the pan from the heat. Stir in the pecans and the
lemon extract. Stir for 5 minutes.

Pour the candy into the prepared pan. When it is completely
cool, cut it into squares.

Pralines

A praline studded with pecans is a perennial favorite. If you like large patties, drop the pralines from a tablespoon. If you prefer them smaller, use a teaspoon. When the pralines have cooled completely, they may be stored in an airtight container between layers of waxed paper.

4 cups firmly packed light brown sugar
$\frac{2}{3}$ cup half-and-half
2 tablespoons unsalted butter
$\frac{1}{8}$ teaspoon salt
2 cups coarsely chopped pecans

Spread a large sheet of waxed paper on a work surface.

In a large, heavy saucepan combine the sugar, half-and-half, butter, and salt. Cook over high heat, stirring constantly until the sugar is dissolved.

Reduce the heat to moderate and continue cooking, without stirring, until the mixture comes to a boil. In the meantime, fill with water a pan into which the saucepan will fit. Bring the water to a boil, then turn off the heat.

When the mixture comes to a boil, begin stirring constantly. Boil for 4 minutes, then stir in the nuts.

Put the saucepan over the hot water while dropping the candy from a spoon onto the waxed paper.

Peppermint Creams

These creamy candies look quite pretty when red or green food coloring is added.

> 2 cups granulated sugar
> $\frac{1}{4}$ cup light corn syrup
> $\frac{1}{4}$ cup milk
> $\frac{1}{4}$ teaspoon cream of tartar
> $\frac{1}{2}$ teaspoon peppermint flavoring
> Red or green food coloring

Spread a large sheet of waxed paper on a work surface.

In a heavy saucepan, combine the sugar, corn syrup, milk, and cream of tartar. Cook over low heat, stirring constantly, until the sugar is dissolved.

Increase the heat to moderate and continue cooking, stirring constantly, until the mixture reaches the soft-ball stage (238°F on a candy thermometer). Remove the pan from the heat and set aside for about 3 minutes to allow the mixture to cool slightly.

Beat in the peppermint and a few drops of food coloring. Continue beating until the mixture is creamy.

Drop the candy by teaspoonfuls onto the waxed paper.

Fudge Favorites

Everyone loves fudge, and here is a collection of marvelous fudge recipes. There's old-fashioned chocolate fudge, penuche, fruit fudge, an unusual banana walnut fudge, never-fail recipes for creamy chocolate pecan fudge and butterscotch walnut fudge, and a rich mocha fudge that requires no cooking.

When making any old-fashioned fudge, use a candy thermometer and be sure to watch the temperatures carefully. When the mixture reaches the boiling point, it becomes very sensitive to stirring and beating. Follow the recipes carefully and success is ensured.

Old-Fashioned Chocolate Fudge

This traditional, rich chocolate fudge is not difficult to make. Just follow the instructions carefully and be sure to use a candy thermometer.

2 ounces unsweetened chocolate
1 cup milk
2 cups granulated sugar
1 tablespoon light corn syrup
2 tablespoons unsalted butter, at room temperature
1 teaspoon vanilla extract
$\frac{1}{2}$ cup finely chopped walnuts

Grease an 8-inch square pan with butter.

In a large, heavy saucepan, combine the chocolate and the milk. Cook over low heat, stirring constantly, until the chocolate has melted and the mixture is smooth.

Stir in the sugar and corn syrup. Increase the heat to moderate and continue stirring until the mixture comes to a boil.

Cover the pan and cook for 1 minute. Uncover the pan and insert a candy thermometer. Cook, uncovered, without stirring, until the mixture reaches the soft-ball stage (236°F on the candy thermometer).

Remove the pan from the heat and stir in the butter and the vanilla. Set aside until the candy cools to lukewarm (110°F).

With a wooden spoon, beat the fudge until it is thick and creamy and no longer glossy. Quickly stir in the nuts.

Pour the fudge into the prepared pan. Cool in the pan on a wire rack.

When the fudge is firm and completely cool, cut it into squares.

Penuche

A brown-sugar fudge studded with pecans, penuche has a creamy texture and caramel flavor.

2 cups firmly packed dark brown sugar
$\frac{3}{4}$ cup milk
$\frac{1}{8}$ teaspoon salt
$\frac{1}{4}$ cup unsalted butter, at room temperature
1 teaspoon vanilla extract
1 cup coarsely chopped pecans

Grease an 8-inch square pan with butter.

In a large, heavy saucepan, combine the sugar, milk, and salt. Cook over moderate heat, stirring constantly, until the mixture comes to a boil. Continue cooking, without stirring, to the soft-ball stage (236°F on the candy thermometer).

Remove the pan from the heat and stir in the butter and the vanilla. Set aside until the candy cools to lukewarm (110°F).

With a wooden spoon, beat the fudge until it becomes thick and begins to lose its gloss. Quickly stir in the pecans.

Pour the fudge into the prepared pan. Cool in the pan on a wire rack.

When the fudge is firm and completely cool, cut it into squares.

Fruit Fudge

This is an old recipe, but it is always successful. Candied cherries may be substituted for the mixed fruit.

2 cups granulated sugar
1 cup milk
$\frac{1}{4}$ cup unsalted butter
1 teaspoon vanilla extract
$\frac{1}{2}$ cup mixed candied fruit, coarsely chopped

Grease an 8-inch square pan with butter.

In a large, heavy saucepan, combine the sugar, milk, and butter. Cook over high heat, stirring constantly, until the sugar is dissolved. Reduce the heat to moderate and continue to cook, stirring constantly, until the mixture comes to a boil.

Cover the pan and cook for 1 minute. Uncover the pan and insert a candy thermometer. Cook, uncovered, without stirring, until the mixture reaches the soft-ball stage (236°F on the candy thermometer).

Remove the pan from the heat and stir in the vanilla. Set aside until the candy cools to lukewarm (110°F).

With a wooden spoon, beat the fudge until it is thick and creamy and is no longer glossy. Quickly stir in the fruit.

Pour the fudge into the prepared pan. Cool in the pan on a wire rack.

When the fudge is firm and completely cool, cut it into squares.

Banana Walnut Fudge

This firm fudge is nicely spiced with cinnamon. It is an old and unusual recipe. A candy thermometer will ensure success.

2 large, ripe bananas
2½ cups granulated sugar
½ cup firmly packed dark brown sugar
1 cup milk
½ teaspoon cream of tartar
2 tablespoons unsalted butter
¼ teaspoon salt
½ teaspoon ground cinnamon
1 teaspoon vanilla extract
1 cup coarsely chopped walnuts

Grease an 8-inch square pan with butter. Mash the bananas.

In a large, heavy saucepan, combine the mashed bananas, sugars, milk, cream of tartar, butter, salt, and cinnamon. Cook over moderate heat, stirring occasionally, until the mixture reaches 226°F on a candy thermometer. Then stir constantly until it reaches the soft-ball stage (236°F).

Remove the pan from the heat and stir in the vanilla. Using a wooden spoon, beat the fudge only until it starts to become creamy and is no longer glossy. Stir in the nuts.

Quickly spread the fudge in the prepared pan. Cool in the pan on a wire rack.

While the fudge is slightly warm, cut it into squares.

Creamy Chocolate Pecan Fudge

This creamy fudge never fails, and it is very easy to make. It will keep best well-covered in the refrigerator.

  7 ounce jar marshmallow cream
  1½ cups granulated sugar
  ⅔ cup evaporated milk
  ¼ cup unsalted butter
  ¼ teaspoon salt
  3 cups semisweet chocolate chips
  1 teaspoon vanilla extract
  1 cup coarsely chopped pecans

Line an 8-inch square pan with foil.

In a large, heavy saucepan, combine the marshmallow cream, sugar, milk, butter, and salt. Bring to a rolling boil over moderate heat, stirring constantly. Boil the mixture, stirring constantly, for 5 minutes.

Remove the pan from the heat and add the chocolate chips, stirring until they have melted and the mixture is smooth. Add the vanilla and the pecans and mix well.

Pour the fudge into the prepared pan. Using a spatula, smooth the top.

Chill in the refrigerator for 2 hours, or until the fudge is firm. Then turn it out of the pan, remove the foil, and cut the fudge into squares.

Butterscotch Walnut Fudge

This butterscotch fudge is very easy to prepare. You don't even need a candy thermometer. The fudge will keep best well-covered in the refrigerator.

   $1\frac{1}{2}$ *cups finely chopped walnuts*
   7 *ounce jar marshmallow cream*
   $1\frac{1}{2}$ *cups granulated sugar*
   $\frac{2}{3}$ *cup evaporated milk*
   $\frac{1}{4}$ *cup unsalted butter*
   $\frac{1}{4}$ *teaspoon salt*
   2 *cups butterscotch chips*

Line an 8-inch square pan with foil. Spread $\frac{3}{4}$ cup of the walnuts in an even layer on the foil.

In a large, heavy saucepan, combine the marshmallow cream, sugar, milk, butter, and salt. Bring to a rolling boil over moderate heat, stirring constantly. Boil the mixture, stirring constantly, for 5 minutes.

Remove the pan from the heat. Stir in the butterscotch chips. Continue to stir until they have melted and the mixture is smooth.

Pour the fudge into the prepared pan and sprinkle the remaining $\frac{3}{4}$ cup of walnuts evenly on top. Using a rubber spatula, gently press the walnuts into the fudge.

Chill in the refrigerator for 2 hours, or until the fudge is firm. Then turn it out of the pan, remove the foil, and cut the fudge into squares.

Mocha Fudge Slices

This rich fudge requires no cooking. Store the slices, layered with waxed paper, in a covered container in the refrigerator. Let them stand at room temperature for about 20 minutes before serving.

  6 ounces unsweetened chocolate
  1 tablespoon instant coffee powder
  2 teaspoons boiling water
  8 ounce package cream cheese, at room temperature
  $\frac{1}{2}$ teaspoon ground cinnamon
  $\frac{1}{8}$ teaspoon salt
  $\frac{1}{4}$ cup coffee liqueur
  5 cups sifted confectioners' sugar
  $2\frac{1}{2}$ cups finely chopped walnuts

In the top of a double boiler, melt the chocolate over barely simmering water, stirring constantly. Remove from the hot water and set aside to cool.

In a small bowl, dissolve the coffee in the boiling water.

In a large mixing bowl, combine the cream cheese, cinnamon, and salt. Beat until the mixture is smooth. Gradually beat in the liqueur and the coffee. Add the melted chocolate and beat until it is well blended. Add the sugar, 1 cup at a time, beating well after each addition. Add 1 cup of nuts and mix well.

Cover the bowl and chill the fudge in the refrigerator for 1 hour, or until it is firm enough to handle.

Spread the remaining $1\frac{1}{2}$ cups of nuts on a cookie sheet.

Divide the fudge into quarters. Working with one quarter at a time, place the fudge in the center of a 12-inch piece of waxed paper. Fold two opposite sides over the fudge. Roll the wrapped fudge into a log about $1\frac{1}{2}$ inches in diameter. Remove the waxed paper and roll the fudge log in the chopped nuts. Wrap each fudge log in plastic wrap and refrigerate overnight, then cut into $\frac{1}{2}$-inch slices.

Christmas Confections

Popcorn balls and taffy apples, candied kumquats and walnut treats, fruit chews and walnut date slices—most of the confections in this section are easy to prepare, and, packaged with imagination, they all make very special, edible gifts.

Popcorn Balls

Popcorn balls are fun to make, especially if there are kids around to help. Make tiny balls and heap them in a bowl. Make medium-size or large balls, wrap each one in cellophane gathered at the top with a red or green ribbon, and hang them on the Christmas tree. About ½ cup of unpopped corn should make the 6 cups of popped corn called for in this recipe.

6 cups popped corn
2 cups shelled peanuts
1½ tablespoons unsalted butter
1¼ cups firmly packed dark brown sugar
6 tablespoons water

Put the popped corn into a large bowl or pot. Add the peanuts. Mix well and set aside.

In a heavy saucepan, melt the butter over low heat. Add the sugar and water and continue cooking over low heat, stirring constantly, until the sugar is dissolved.

Increase the heat to moderate and boil the syrup, without stirring, until it reaches the soft-ball stage (238°F on a candy thermometer).

Slowly pour the hot syrup over the popped corn and peanuts, turning and mixing with a long-handled wooden spoon to coat all the kernels and nuts.

As soon as the mixture is cool enough to handle, shape it lightly into balls with buttered hands.

Let the popcorn balls dry thoroughly on waxed paper or a cookie sheet before wrapping them.

Almond Pecan Popcorn

This nutty popcorn has a light caramel glaze. It makes a wonderful gift, since it keeps well in airtight containers. A scant $\frac{3}{4}$ cup of unpopped corn should make the 8 cups of popped corn called for in this recipe.

2 cups pecan halves
2 cups blanched, whole almonds
8 cups popped corn
2 cups granulated sugar
1 cup light corn syrup
$\frac{2}{3}$ cup water
2 cups unsalted butter, at room temperature

Preheat the oven to 350°F. Lightly oil a large bowl or pot. Lightly grease two cookie sheets with butter.

Spread the pecans and almonds on an ungreased cookie sheet in one layer. Toast them in the oven for about 10 minutes, or until they are lightly browned.

Combine the toasted nuts and the popped corn in the bowl or pot. Mix well.

In a large, heavy saucepan, combine the sugar, corn syrup, and water. Cook over high heat, stirring constantly, until the sugar is dissolved. Reduce the heat to moderate and cook, stirring frequently, until the mixture comes to a boil. Cut the butter into pieces, then add it and continue cooking, stirring constantly, until the mixture reaches the hard-crack stage (300°F on a candy thermometer).

Slowly pour the hot syrup over the nuts and popcorn, mixing and tossing with a long-handled wooden spoon to coat the nuts and popcorn with the caramel. Spread half the popcorn mixture in a thin layer on each cookie sheet.

When the mixture is completely cool, break it into small pieces.

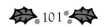

Walnut Treats

These sugary walnuts are flavored with lemon and orange. They will keep well in an airtight container.

1 cup granulated sugar
2 tablespoons water
2 tablespoons orange juice
2 tablespoons grated orange peel
2 tablespoons grated lemon peel
2 cups walnut halves

Grease a cookie sheet with butter.

In a heavy saucepan, combine the sugar, water, and orange juice. Cook over moderate heat, stirring constantly, until the syrup reaches the firm-ball stage (244°F on a candy thermometer).

Remove the pan from the heat and stir in the orange peel, lemon peel, and walnuts. Continue to stir until the syrup is creamy and the walnuts are well coated.

Spread the nuts on the prepared cookie sheet. Be sure they are all separated. Set aside until completely cool.

Fruit Chews

These chewy fruit-nut balls require no cooking and are full of good healthy ingredients. Store them in a cool, dry place or in the refrigerator.

1½ cups raisins
1 cup dried apricots
1 cup pitted dates
1 cup flaked coconut
1 cup finely chopped walnuts

In a food processor or blender, grind the raisins, apricots, and dates.

In a large mixing bowl, combine the ground fruit with the coconut and ½cup of the walnuts. Mix well.

Shape the mixture into thirty 1-inch balls.

Spread the remaining ½ cup of chopped nuts on a plate. Roll the balls in the nuts, pressing the nuts firmly into them.

Walnut Date Slices

This chewy confection is quite easy to make. Pecans may be substituted for the walnuts. The slices keep best well-covered in the refrigerator, but serve them at room temperature.

> 3 cups granulated sugar
> 1 cup evaporated milk
> 1 cup finely chopped pitted dates
> 1 cup finely chopped walnuts

In a heavy saucepan, combine the sugar and milk. Cook over high heat, stirring constantly, until the sugar dissolves. Reduce heat to moderate and continue cooking, and stirring, until the mixture reaches the soft-ball stage (238°F on a candy thermometer).

Remove the pan from the heat and stir in the dates and the walnuts.

When the mixture is cool enough to handle, shape it into a roll, about 2 inches in diameter, using buttered hands. Wrap the roll in plastic wrap. Chill in the refrigerator overnight. Then, using a sharp knife, cut the roll into slices $\frac{1}{4}$ inch thick.

Taffy Apples

Commercially made taffy apples don't compare to the ones you make yourself. Be sure to use well-flavored, unblemished apples.

8 *small or 6 large apples*
2 *cups granulated sugar*
$\frac{1}{2}$ *cup water*
$\frac{1}{8}$ *teaspoon cream of tartar*
$\frac{1}{2}$ *cup unsalted butter, cut into small pieces*
1 *teaspoon white vinegar*
$\frac{1}{2}$ *cup heavy cream*

Push a lollypop stick or a skewer into the stem end of each apple. Liberally grease a cookie sheet with butter.

In a large, heavy saucepan, combine the sugar and the water. Cook over low heat, stirring constantly, until the sugar is dissolved.

Stir in the cream of tartar, butter, vinegar, and cream. Cook, stirring constantly, until the mixture reaches the soft-crack stage (290°F on a candy thermometer). Remove the pan from the heat.

Dip each apple into the syrup, then carefully place it on the prepared cookie sheet.

When the taffy has cooled completely, wrap each apple in plastic wrap.

Candied Orange Peel

This recipe makes a sugary, moist confection that keeps for many weeks in an airtight container. If you prefer candied grapefruit peel to orange, simply substitute the peel of 4 large grapefruits. Do not mix the peels in one batch. It's better to candy them separately.

8 *large unblemished oranges*
3 *cups granulated sugar*
1 *cup water*

Score the peel of each orange into eighths, then, using a blunt knife, pry the peel off the fruit. Scrape as much of the white pith (which can make the candy bitter) as possible from the inside of the peel. Cut the peel into strips.

Put the peel into a saucepan and add cold water to cover. Cook over low heat until the water comes to a boil. Remove the pan from the heat and drain the peel well. Repeat this process four more times, draining the peel thoroughly each time.

In a heavy saucepan, combine 2 cups of the sugar and the water. Cook over high heat, stirring constantly, until the sugar dissolves. Bring the syrup to a boil, add the drained peel, and cook over moderate heat, stirring constantly, until all the syrup is absorbed by the peel.

Turn the peel out onto an ungreased cookie sheet. Separate the peel. Let it cool.

Spread the remaining 1 cup of sugar on a large plate. Put a large sheet of waxed paper on a work surface.

When the peel is cool, roll it in the sugar, then put the pieces on the waxed paper to dry for about 2 hours.

Candied Kumquats

This sweet-sour little fruit has a unique flavor and makes a delightful confection. Use only firm, brightly colored kumquats.

4 cups kumquats
5 cups water
3½ cups granulated sugar
⅛ teaspoon cream of tartar

Wash the kumquats and, using a skewer or a tapestry needle, prick a hole in the stem end of each one.

Put the kumquats into a saucepan and add 4 cups of water. Cook over moderate heat until the water begins to boil. Reduce the heat and simmer the kumquats for 10 minutes.

Drain the kumquats in a colander, then spread them on paper towels to dry.

In a heavy saucepan, combine the remaining cup of water with 2 cups of the sugar. Cook over low heat, stirring constantly, until the sugar is dissolved. Stir in the cream of tartar. Increase the heat to moderate and cook, stirring constantly, until the syrup reaches the soft-ball stage (238°F on a candy thermometer).

Reduce the heat to low, add the kumquats, and let them simmer gently, stirring frequently, for 10 minutes.

Using a perforated spoon, remove the kumquats from the syrup and put them on wire racks to drain and cool.

Spread the remaining 1½ cups of sugar on a plate.

When the kumquats are cool enough to handle, roll each one in the sugar. Return the kumquats to the wire racks to cool completely.